British History

CASTLES & KNIGHTS

Philip Steele

MILES KELLY
PUBLISHING

First published in 2002 by Miles Kelly Publishing Ltd,
Bardfield Centre, Great Bardfield, Essex, CM7 4SL

ISBN 1-84236-466-9

2 4 6 8 10 9 7 5 3

Some material in this book can also be found
in the *Encyclopedia of British History*

Editorial Director: Belinda Gallagher
Project Manager: Kate Miles
Art Director: Jo Brewer
Picture Researcher: Liberty Newton
Production Manager: Elizabeth Brunwin

Contact us by email: info@mileskelly.net
Website: www.mileskelly.net

Printed in China

CONTENTS

INTRODUCTION

Massive stone castles still tower over the landscapes of the British Isles, guarding lonely mountain passes, valleys and coasts and towering over market towns that today are peaceful and quiet. They are a reminder us of the violent years of the high Middle Ages.

Knights were often away for long periods of time fighting in the crusades.

Ladies sitting in their beautiful finery watch their knights compete in jousting tournaments.

were often prepared to use it even against members of their own family. Challenges to royal rule from other sections of society came in the form of violent uprisings, the limiting of royal power through laws and the development of parliaments. England, Wales and Scotland began to emerge as united countries.

Castle-building was brought to the islands by the Normans, the descendants of Vikings who had settled in France. They conquered England in 1066, and were soon carving out lordships on the Welsh borders, settling in southern Scotland and invading Ireland. The most important Norman soldiers were armed horsemen, and these 'knights' soon became powerful members of society.

The Middle Ages were troubled times, when the common people suffered greatly from hunger and disease and were forced to toil on the land. Kings ruled their lands with force and

Noble families sought power through marriage alliances, and royal marriages brought the English kings and queens vast new territories in France. England was the growing power, almost perpetually at war with the French, the Welsh and Scots. It was also trying to bring Ireland under its control. Wales suffered defeat in 1283, but England was at last forced to recognize Scottish independence in 1328.

All the countries of the British Isles saw themselves as part of Christendom, a Europe united by the Christian faith and headed by the Pope in Rome. Christian knights repeatedly went to war against Islamic armies in the Near East and in Spain.

Christian monks and nuns were engaged in teaching and caring for the sick, and in copying out beautiful, illustrated texts by hand. New inventions entered Europe from Asia, along with imported silks and spices. The first universities were founded. Languages of the British Isles, such as English, Welsh, Scots and

Castles were often under threat of seige and needed a ready army of soldiers to defend against attack.

Irish Gaelic, began to take on forms we can recognize today, and be used more widely, alongside Latin and Norman French.

Poetry and literature flourished, and many of the texts glorified the life of the knights and their ladies and the code of honour they were supposed to follow. This ideal of 'chivalry' was never more than a dream, but it was one which would inspire many future generations in the British Isles.

The castle kitchens were always busy preparing food for the lords and ladies being entertained upstairs.

CASTLES AND KNIGHTS

AD1066–1509

THE WORLD AT A GLANCE

ELSEWHERE IN EUROPE

1220
King Frederick II of Sicily and Germany becomes Holy Roman Emperor

1226
Louis IX (St Louis) comes to the throne in France

1237
Mongol armies invade East and Central Europe (to 1241)

1378
A split in the Roman Church, with one Pope in Rome and another in Avignon, France

1453
Turks capture Constantinople (Istanbul). End of the Byzantine empire

1462
Lorenzo de Medici rules over splendid court at Florence, Italy

1480
Ivan the Great, first Tsar of Russia, expels the Mongols and unites his country

1492
Christians finally reconquer all of Moslem Spain, rule of Ferdinand and Isabella

ASIA

1096
European Crusaders attack Moslems in the Near East and found Christian kingdoms

1170
The Hindu Srivijaya kingdom rules Java, Southeast Asia

1190
Temujin (Genghis Khan) starts to create the Mongol empire

1192
Yoritomo Minamoto becomes first Shogun (military dictator) in Japan

1206
The Islamic Sultanate rules in Delhi, India

1271
Mongol ruler Kublai Khan becomes the emperor of China

1368
Ming emperors rule China, capital at Nanjing

1405
Death of Timur the Lame (or Tamberlaine), Tatar ruler of a vast Asian empire

AFRICA

1200
The rise of the state of Mali in West Africa

1200
Rise of Hausa city-states in northern Nigeria and Kanem-Bornu in Lake Chad region

1250
Rise of the Benin empire in southern Nigerian forests

1250
High stone enclosures built at Great Zimbabwe, in southeast Africa

1300
Founding of the Kongo kingdom in southern Central Africa

1400
Chinese, Arab and Indian traders along East Africa's Swahili Coast

1400
Fine heads made from bronze in the Benin empire

1450
Height of Songhai power in southern Sahara, university at Timbuktu

"The peasant toils, the king rules – and God is in His heaven…"

Llywelyn Fawr

NORTH AMERICA

1100
Thule culture of the American Arctic, based on whaling

1150
The Anasazi people settle Mesa Verde in the southwest

1170
Collapse of Toltec rule in Mexico, period of wars and strife

1300
The Maya people return to power in Mexico, with capital at Mayapán

1345
Aztecs build the great city of Teotihuacan on the modern site of Mexico City

1428
The Aztec empire expands and becomes very powerful

1492
Christopher Columbus, in the service of Spain, lands in the Caribbean

1493
The Spanish settle on the Caribbean island of Hispaniola

SOUTH AMERICA

1100
The city of Cuzco, Peru, is founded by the first Inca emperor

1370
The Chimú empire expands in northern Peru

1450
The founding of the Inca town of Machu Picchu, high in the Andes

1470
The Incas conquer the Chimú empire

1492
The Incas conquer northern Chile

1493
The Treaty of Tordesillas. Spain and Portugal divide up the Americas.

1498
The Inca empire is at its greatest extent under ruler Wayna Qapaq

1500
The Portuguese claim Brazil

OCEANIA

1100
Increased farming and irrigation begins on the Hawaiian islands

1200
Powerful chiefdoms grow up in Polynesia

1200
The Tu'i Tonga dynasty rules the Tongan Islands and part of Samoa

1200
Large numbers of stone platforms and houses built in the Society Islands

1250
Funeral of the Melanesian ruler Roy Mata on the island of Retoka

1300
Giant moa is hunted to extinction in New Zealand, increase in agriculture

1350
Classic Maori period begins on New Zealand, large fortresses

1400s
Malay fishermen camp on shores of northern Australia

10

✤ 1064
Harold swears to support
William of Normandy

✤ 1066
Harold II chosen as King of
England

✤ 1066
King Harald III of Norway
defeated at Stamford Bridge

✤ 1066
Norman invasion. Harold II
defeated at Battle of Hastings

✤ 1067
William I starts to build the
Tower of London

HASTIΠGS 1066

WHO WERE THE NORMANS?

The Anglo-Saxon kings were not the only ones who attempted buy off the Vikings. In AD 911 Charles 'the Simple', King of France, offered a Viking warlord called Rollo part of northern France in a desperate bid to win peace. It became called Normandy ('land of the Northmen'). Rollo became a duke and married Giselle, a French princess. Like their Viking ancestors, Norman warlords stormed their way around Europe. They invaded the Italian island of Sicily in 1060.

I N the summer of 1066 a large fleet assembled along the French coast. Its commander was William, Duke of Normandy. Ships wallowed at anchor in choppy seas, waiting for the northerly wind to turn. Norman lords galloped to and fro on horseback. Carts trundled along the beach loaded with spears, swords, arrows and axes, iron helmets, shields and coats of mail. This would be the last major invasion of England in the Middle Ages.

Archers
The bow used by the Normans was about 1.5 metres long and was drawn to the chest. It was said that a Norman arrow pierced King Harold's eye and killed him.

Wooden weapons
Bows were made of elm, but arrows of ash. The flights were made from goose feathers.

The Battle of Hastings remains the most famous event in English history. Its shockwaves were felt right across the British Isles.

CLAIMS FOR THE THRONE

Harold of Wessex was the son of a powerful Anglo-Saxon earl called Godwin. In January 1066 the Witan named Harold as King of England, but their decision was challenged at once. Edward the Ætheling, nephew of Edward the Confessor, claimed the throne. So did Harold's own brother, Tostig. A third claimant was King Harald III of Norway, known as 'Hardraade', 'the Ruthless'. The fourth was William of Normandy. William swore that in 1064 Harold had made a solemn vow to support the Norman claim.

RULERS OF ENGLAND	
House of Normandy	
✤ William I 'the Conqueror'	1066–1087
✤ William II 'Rufus'	1087–1100
✤ Henry I 'Beauclerk'	1100–1135
✤ Stephen	1135–1154

✤ 1068
Norman conquest of
northern and western England

✤ 1069
Anglo-Saxon uprising, led by
Edward the Ætheling

✤ 1070
Rebellion in East Anglia by
Hereward 'the Wake'

✤ 1085
William I orders compilation
of the Domesday Book

✤ 1087
War with France, William I
dies after he falls from horse

11

ONE BATTLE TOO MANY

Harold II's troops were waiting for the Normans when word
came that Harald III of Norway had joined forces with Tostig.
Harold marched northwards at speed. He defeated and killed
them both at Stamford Bridge, near York. Just three days later,
Norman troops landed in Sussex. Harold had to march his
exhausted army south again. On 14 October 1066, the two
great armies clashed at Senlac Hill, near Hastings. All day, wave
after wave of Normans broke against the Anglo-Saxon shields.
Harold's men stood firm but, scenting victory, they broke rank
too soon. The victory belonged to William – 'the Conqueror'.

THE DOMESDAY BOOK

Exactly 19 years after his
coronation, William I
announced that all the lands in
England south of the rivers
Ribble and Tees (and
excluding the cities of London
and Winchester) were to be
registered in a great book.
From 1086 onwards, royal
officials travelled from one
estate to another. They wrote
down the details of buildings,
land and resources, so that
they could be taxed.

Shield
The long kite-shaped
shield was developed
by the Norman cavalry

Helmet
The iron, cone-shaped
helmet was worn over a
hood of mail, called a coif.

*This tapestry of wool on a linen
backing has a 70-metre long 'strip'
format, which tells the story of the Norman
invasion of England. It can still be seen
today in Bayeux, Normandy.*

**Coats
of mail**
Norman warriors protected
themselves with a mail shirt
worn over a tunic.

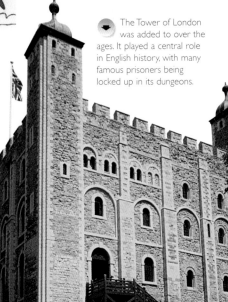

*The Tower of London
was added to over the
ages. It played a central role
in English history, with many
famous prisoners being
locked up in its dungeons.*

THE CONQUEST

On Christmas Day 1066, William I was crowned
king in Westminster Abbey. Within months of his
coronation, William ordered the building of a new
fortification by the River Thames, in London. Its
great keep, or stronghold, was the White Tower.
This became the centre of the Tower of London.

Within two years most of England was under his
control. Revolts led by Edward the Ætheling and
an Anglo-Saxon lord called Hereward the Wake
('the Watchful') were crushed.

12

✤ 1066
The Norman Channel Islands
come under the English crown

✤ 1072
William I of England leads
army into Scotland

✤ 1092
Normans build castle at
Pembroke in South Wales

✤ 1094
'Marcher' Lordships
established in the Welsh
borders

✤ 1094
Norman invasion
of North Wales

THE MAILED FIST

THE Norman kings of England and their successors wanted to be recognized as overlords of all the British Isles. Their fleets sailed north and their armies were soon battling with the Scots. Norman warlords were given territories on the Welsh borders (the 'Marches'), and stormed into North and South Wales. Within a hundred years, their great castles of stone could be seen in Ireland, too.

Braided hair
Norman ladies
often wore their
hair in plaits. Heads
were sometimes
covered with a
short veil, secured
by a circlet of silver
or gold.

◀ *Dermot, the Irish ruler of Leinster, needed the support of Strongbow (right). In return he offered him the hand of his daughter, Aoife, and succession to the throne of Leinster*

A cloak
A long woollen
cloak was worn for
warmth, fastened
across the front by
a cord.

The girdle
A cord or jewelled
belt was worn
around the waist.

A flowing dress
A long-sleeved shift was
covered by a long tunic
called a bliaut, which
was laced at the side.

◀ *A Norman lady*

THE NORMANS IN SCOTLAND

After repeated Scottish invasions of his new kingdom, William I marched into Lothian at the head of a large army in 1071, but he made peace with Malcolm Canmore at Abernethy. In 1092 the Normans took Cumbria from the Scots, but a full-scale invasion of Scotland never occurred. Norman settlers did arrive, bringing their ways to the Lowlands and to the Scottish court. Later Scottish kings, including Robert Bruce and the Stewarts, were of Norman descent.

Supplies
Weapons and equipment
had to be carried with the
troops. Food and grain
could be seized by force
along the way.

✤ 1097
Normans defeat
Donald III of
Scotland

✤ 1100
William II of England is killed,
possibly murdered, in the
New Forest

✤ 1106
Henry I of England defeats
and imprisons his brother
Robert in Normandy

✤ 1166
Dermot MacMurrough of
Leinster invites Normans into
Ireland

✤ 1170
Normans invade from
Baginbun, Wexford

13

WALES AND THE MARCHES

The Norman kings did not intend to rule Wales directly, but they wished to control it. As early as 1067 William I gave land on the borders to William Fitzosbern, Roger Montgomery and Hugh d'Avranches. These 'Marcher Lords' were a law to themselves. They launched savage raids into North Wales in the 1080s. By the 1090s Norman warlords were gaining control of large areas of South and West Wales. They met fierce resistance, but this was a period when the Welsh kingdoms were at war with each other. The Normans were defeated in 1096 at Gelli Carnant, Gwent, but they kept their foothold in Wales.

GWENLLIAN GOES TO WAR

Gwenllian was the daughter of Gruffudd ap Cynan, ruler of Gwynedd in North Wales. She married another Grufudd, son of Rhys ap Tewdwr, ruler of Deheubarth. In 1136 her husband went to meet her father, to plan a rising against the Normans in South Wales. While he was away, Gwenllian led a warrior band to storm Kidwelly castle. They were beaten back and defeated by Maurice de Londres. Gwenllian was killed in the attack.

Horse power
The Normans used highly mobile forces to control their conquests.

Metal in motion
The mounted knight was the key to Norman success.

STRONGBOW'S IRELAND

In Ireland, warring between provincial kings gave a chance for descendants of the Normans to invade. In 1166 Dermot MacMurrough, King of Leinster, appealed to Henry II of England for help. He had lost his lands in the wars between Ireland's provincial kings. Henry authorised Norman lords to carry on this fight independently.

In 1169 Richard fitz Gilbert de Clare, Earl of Pembroke, agreed to help Dermot in return for land. De Clare, half Norman and half Welsh, was known as 'Strongbow'. His invasion of Ireland was successful – too much so for Henry II, who was jealous of Strongbow's new-found power. The English king and his army arrived in Ireland in 1171.

 The Norman invasion did not stop at the borders of England.

14

✤ **1086**
Population of 2 million in area surveyed by the Domesday Book

✤ **1086**
Domesday Book records over 2 million hectares of land as cultivated

✤ **1191**
First record of windmills being used for grinding wheat

✤ **1200s**
Rapid growth of towns and cities

✤ **1300s**
Feudal system begins to be replaced by a money-based economy

THE FEUDAL SYSTEM

THE division of society into classes of serfs, free men, nobles and rulers had started earlier in the Middle Ages. The Normans were the first to enforce this 'feudal' system rigidly. The king was at the top, ruling by the will of God. He parcelled out land to his lords in return for their support. The land was worked by free men and serfs (or 'villeins'), who provided the nobles with food and served in their armies. In return, the poor were, in theory at least, protected by their lord.

Kings of the Middle Ages held extreme power over their subjects. Every royal document was marked with a personal badge called a seal, pressed into soft wax. This one belonged to Henry I of England.

OATHS OF LOYALTY

The feudal system was a series of two-way contracts, reinforced by oaths of loyalty. The loyalty was not to a nation, but to a noble or royal family. A lord could even insist that 'his' people take up arms against their own countrymen. The feudal system crossed national borders. Europe's ruling classes were allied with each other, rather than with the peasants who worked for them. If a king from one royal family married the princess of another, the lands they ruled might be joined together, regardless of public opinion or geography.

Field use
One field might be for oats and another for wheat. The third might lie 'fallow' (uncultivated) and be grazed by cattle. Field use changed from year to year so that the goodness in the soil was not all used up.

The feudal economy was based on land and services rather than money. It only worked if people stayed on the land. Villeins were not allowed to leave their village and were forced to work on their lord's estates.

✤ **1300s**
Rise of a middle class made up of merchants and craft producers

✤ **1300s**
Cloth production moves out of towns, water power needed for fulling

✤ **1300s**
Spinning wheels introduced into the British Isles

✤ **c1330**
The *Luttrell Psalter* includes illustrations of everyday English life

✤ **1349**
Ordinance of Labourers tries to limit English wages

15

WOMEN IN THE MIDDLE AGES

In the medieval (Middle Ages) period, most women in Europe had few rights. Strict vows bound together man and wife, just as society was bound by oaths of feudal loyalty. It was the men who held real power and wealth. Despite this, many women were strong characters and became widely respected in their own right. There were powerful queens and noblewomen, abbesses and nuns, scholars and poets, and able working women in every village. In the later Middle Ages, poets began to sing the praises of women, but in a very idealized way.

Women may have been honoured in medieval poetry but in reality had hard lives. Many died in childbirth.

RICH AND POOR

The Norman lords who had supported William I during the invasion of England profited hugely. They were rather like the lottery winners of today, only their new-found wealth was based on land rather than money. This created problems for kings that followed, for there were now many very powerful lords who could challenge their rule. At the other end of the scale were the villeins. They had to labour on the lord's land for, say, three days a week. They also had to pay taxes and supply farm produce to the lord. The Church too demanded one-tenth (a 'tithe') of their harvested crops.

Windmill
Windmills, originally an Asian invention, were first built in Britain during the 1190s. They were mounted on an upright post, and could be turned so that the sails caught the wind. They were used for grinding grain into flour.

Harrow
A harrow was a spiked frame used for preparing the soil ready for the seeds to be scattered by the sower.

16

✤ 1100
Death of William II of England,
called 'Rufus'

✤ 1106
Battle of Tinchebrai. Henry I
regains Normandy

✤ 1120
Prince William, heir to the
English throne, is drowned

✤ 1135
Stephen is crowned English
king. Start of civil war

✤ 1148
Matilda leaves England,
Stephen rules

IS MIGHT RIGHT?

IN the days of William the Conqueror, life was short and violent. The road to kingship was not through election or consent. It was often through murder and battle. Even the laws reflected the belief that 'might is right'. A legal dispute might be settled by an official fight – 'trial by combat' – or by making the accused grasp a red hot bar of iron – 'trial by ordeal'. God, it was believed, would punish the guilty and protect the innocent.

A KING'S NIGHTMARES

In 1100, William II of England was killed in a hunting accident in the New Forest. Or was it murder? Nobody knew for sure. Six years later his successor, Henry I, imprisoned his own brother for 28 years. A series of pictures drawn in the 1140s shows Henry I haunted by royal nightmares. Haughty bishops, armed knights and angry peasants all protest by his bedside.

Armed might invades the peace of Canterbury Cathedral in 1170. Four knights have burst in to murder English archbishop Thomas Becket while he prays.

THE FIGHTING EMPRESS

When Henry I's son was drowned at sea in 1120, he named his daughter Matilda as his heir. She lived in Germany at that time, for she had been betrothed (engaged to be married) at the age of just seven to the Emperor Henry V. She had married him in 1114, aged twelve. Widowed in 1125, Matilda soon remarried another very powerful but younger man, Geoffrey of Anjou. She fought desperately for the English throne until 1148.

Matilda flees from Oxford. She was unpopular with the English people. At one time she captured Stephen, but was never crowned queen.

A TIME OF TERROR

Henry I did manage to keep order in the land, but after his death in 1135, there was chaos. Before his chosen heir, Matilda, arrived back in England, the throne was seized by Stephen, a grandson of William I. There followed 13 years of war between the two. It was a terrible period for the common people, as lord fought lord and armies looted the land.

✤1154
Henry II comes to throne, legal reform

✤1170
Murder of Thomas Becket, Archbishop of Canterbury

✤1215
Barons force King John to sign *Magna Carta*

✤1258
Henry III hands over power to a council of barons

✤1265
De Montfort calls the first English parliament

17

TRIAL BY JURY

A fairer legal system was brought in by Henry II of England during the 1100s. Punishments for crimes were still often brutal, but now courts were held around the country in the king's name. Juries were called to decide guilt or innocence. In those days, juries were not independent members of the public but people who may have known the accused or witnessed the crime.

BISHOPS AND BARONS

The Roman Church was very powerful. Popes believed that as God's representatives they had the right to control European politics. Quarrels between kings and the Church became common. In 1170 supporters of Henry II of England murdered Thomas Becket, the Archbishop of Canterbury. Another challenge to royal power came from barons (powerful nobles). In 1215 English barons forced King John to agree to recognize their legal rights. The agreement was known as *Magna Carta* ('the great charter'). The barons did not need protection, but at least the law was now recognized as more important than the word of kings and queens.

King John was a weak ruler. In 1215, at Runnymede, near the River Thames, he caved in to the demands of his rebel barons and signed the Magna Carta.

A SUMMONS TO PARLIAMENT

Magna Carta may have been one of the first moves towards social justice, but its immediate effect was to make the warring barons even more powerful. When Henry III of England came to the throne in 1216, he was only a child. In 1258 he was forced to hand over power to the barons.

Their leader was Simon de Montfort, Earl of Leicester and brother-in-law of the king. He imprisoned Henry III at Lewes, Sussex, in 1264. The next year de Montfort called a great council, or 'parliament'. Each county sent a knight and each town sent a burgess (leading citizen).

De Montfort was killed in 1265, but parliaments were again summoned by later kings. By 1352 parliament had two sections or 'chambers'. The House of Lords was for the nobles and the bishops, while the House of Commons was for knights and burgesses.

18

✣ 1128
Matilda marries Geoffrey
of Anjou

✣ 1152
Henry of Anjou marries
Eleanor of Aquitaine

✣ 1154
Henry II is crowned first
Plantagenet king of England

✣ c1167
Students start to
study at Oxford

✣ 1198
Richard I 'Cœur de Lion' dies
from a crossbow wound

THE ANGEVIN EMPIRE

ALTHOUGH Matilda failed to win the throne of England, her son was crowned King Henry II in 1154. His royal line is sometimes called Plantagenet, named after the sprig of broom (in Old French, *plante genêt*) that his father Geoffrey wore in his cap. Henry II ruled over a huge area of western Europe called the Angevin (Anjou) empire.

WHICH LANGUAGE?

The English spoken today began to take shape in medieval England. It grew out of several languages. The court used French, while scholars and the Church used Latin. Most ordinary people spoke dialects of English. Other languages spoken in the British Isles at this time included Cornish, Welsh, Scots Gaelic, Irish and Norse.

THE ANGEVIN EMPIRE

inherited through Henry's father

under direct rule

owing allegiance

Acquisitions by marriage with Eleanor

under direct rule

owing allegiance

other acquisitions 1169-72

control by marriage of Geoffrey with Constance of Brittany

unsuccessfully claimed

Kingdom of France

SCOTLAND
IRELAND
WALES
ENGLAND
London
NORTH SEA
ENGLISH CHANNEL
Normandy
Paris
Brittany
Anjou
FRANCE
Poitou
Bourges
Aquitaine
Bordeaux
Gascony
Toulouse
Béarne

ROYAL LANDS

Henry II's lands stretched from the sunny vineyards of Bordeaux in southwest France, to the rainy Scottish borders. He had inherited Anjou from his father and gained Poitou, Aquitaine and Gascony on marrying Eleanor of Aquitaine. Henry also claimed to be overlord of Brittany, Wales, Scotland and Ireland.

THE EMPIRE UNRAVELS

Henry II of England was energetic and fiery-tempered. He was a very able ruler, but he quarrelled bitterly with his wife and with his sons. They rebelled against him and the great empire began to break up. Royal power lessened under Stephen and John, but the struggle to control France would continue for hundreds of years.

RULERS OF ENGLAND
House of Anjou (Plantagenet)

✣ Henry II 'Curtmantle'	1154-1189
✣ Richard I 'Cœur de Lion'	1189-1199
✣ John 'Lackland'	1199-1216
✣ Henry III	1216-1272
✣ Edward I 'Longshanks'	1272-1307
✣ Edward II	1307-1327
✣ Edward III 'of Windsor'	1327-1377
✣ Richard II	1377-1399

✤ **1205**
England loses Normandy to
France

✤ **1215**
Cambridge University is
founded

✤ **1267**
Opus Majus ('great work')
by Roger Bacon

✤ **1283**
First record of a mechanical
clock in England

✤ **1326**
First record of spectacles
being used in England

19

ELEANOR OF AQUITAINE

Eleanor of Aquitaine was one of the most remarkable women in medieval Europe. She was born in about 1122. She became Duchess of Aquitaine in 1135, when she married the heir to the French throne. He was crowned Louis VII two years later. Eleanor was unconventional and beautiful. She and a troop of women, dressed as classical warriors, joined the Second Crusade (one of the wars between Christians and Moslems in the Near East). After her marriage was annulled (cancelled) in 1152, Eleanor married young Henry of Anjou, who became King Henry II of England. Their love soon turned sour and when Henry was unfaithful she supported his sons in rebellion against him. She was imprisoned from 1174 until the death of Henry in 1189. She died in 1204.

◗ The lute was widely played in western Europe in the Middle Ages. Musicians performed at court and poets and singers travelled from one castle to another.

◗ Eleanor's court in Poitou attracted poets, musicians and scholars from all over Europe.

SCHOLARS AND INVENTORS

Under Plantagenet rule in England, few people could read or write. Some children were taught in church schools or were tutored by monks or nuns. University students may have been studying at Oxford as early as 1167, and Cambridge University was founded in 1215. One scholar who studied at Oxford and Paris was Roger Bacon (c1214–1292). He was a scientist who predicted the use of flying machines and telescopes. At this time all sorts of exciting new inventions were arriving in Britain from abroad, including gunpowder, clocks and spectacles.

FOOD FOR A ROYAL BANQUET

England's medieval language divide has survived in the kitchen today. English-speakers raised 'sheep', but the French-speaking nobles who ate them called them '*moutons*'. 'Mutton' later became used for the cooked meat.

Medieval feasts or banquets included huge pies and tarts, jellies, fish such as eels and lampreys, roast goose or swan and venison. Dishes were served with great ceremony.

◗ boar's head

20

✤ AD 632
Death of Muhammad, founder
of Islam, in Arabia

✤ 1075
Moslem Turks capture the holy
city of Jerusalem

✤ 1095
Pope Urban II calls for a holy
war or 'Crusade'

✤ 1096
The First Crusade leaves
Europe for the Holy Land

✤ 1099
Crusaders capture Jerusalem,
massacre 40,000 Jews and
Moslems

THE CRUSADES

IN 1075 the city of Jerusalem was captured from its Christian rulers by Turkish Moslems. Twenty years later, Pope Urban II appealed to all Christian knights to launch a holy war, or Crusade. Its aim was to recapture Jerusalem and the 'Holy Land'. The First Crusade began in 1096 and Jerusalem was taken after three long years.

Moslem lands stretched from Spain through North Africa to Southwest Asia. The Christian lands of Europe were known as Christendom. The Christian lands of the Near East were called Outremer ('overseas').

JEWS, CHRISTIANS, MOSLEMS

By now, most of Europe was Christian. The Moors (Moslem Berbers and Arabs) had conquered much of Spain, but were under constant attack by Christian armies from the north. There were communities of Jews in many parts of Europe, too. Their ancestors had been expelled from Jerusalem by the Romans in AD 70. In Moorish Spain, Moslems, Christians and Jews lived peaceably together. However in most of Christendom, religious hatred against Moslems and Jews ran rife. Jews were persecuted terribly in England and in 1290 they were expelled by Edward I.

RICHARD THE LION HEART

One of the most famous English kings, Richard I spent only 10 months of his reign in England and probably spoke only French. In 1189 he became King of England. In the following year he joined the Third Crusade, at first with King Philippe Auguste of France. In 1191 he captured the city of Acre. Richard's exploits brought him fame and the nickname *Cœur de Lion* ('Lion Heart'). Journeying home,

Richard was shipwrecked and forced to cross the lands of his enemy, Duke Leopold of Austria. He was captured and handed over to Emperor Henry VI. A huge sum ('a ransom') had to be paid for his release and it was the English people who had to find the money. Richard was killed fighting against France in 1199.

Richard I, son of Henry I and Eleanor of Aquitaine, spent most of his reign at war.

✤ **1099**
Christian kingdom founded at Jerusalem

✤ **1148**
The Second Crusade fails to capture Damascus in Syria

✤ **1189**
The Third Crusade is launched, Richard I pledges support

✤ **1202**
Crusaders attack the Christian city of Constantinople

✤ **1291**
The fall of Acre, end of crusading against the Saracens

21

The Crusader
Crusaders were armed with swords, lances, axes and maces. Their armour varied over the years. Chain mail gave way to solid plate armour.

RELIGIOUS WARS

There were several further Crusades between 1096 and 1270. These shameful wars poisoned relations between Christianity and Islam into modern times. Religious motives soon gave way to looting and land-grabbing. Moslems were not the only enemy. In 1204, Crusaders turned aside to sack the Christian city of Constantinople. In 1208 a Crusade was launched against Christians in southern France, who differed from Rome in their beliefs. German Crusaders invaded Poland and the Baltic lands in the 1200s.

Saracen weapons
The Saracens had swords of the finest steel, spears and round shields. Archers fired arrows from small bows while riding.

Saracen armour
Moslem troops either wore tunics which were padded or sewn with metal plates, or coats of mail.

◀ Fighting in the dry heat and dust of the Near East, when weighed down with armour and weapons, was often an ordeal. Although the Crusades were meant to be 'holy' wars, the citizens of besieged towns were often slaughtered without mercy. The Crusades left a bitterness between Christianity and Islam that still affects the politics of Southwest Asia today.

CRUSADERS AND SARACENS

Crusaders came from all over Europe, including the British Isles. Some joined international 'orders', such as the Knights of St John (founded in 1099), or the Knights Templar (1119). The Moslem soldiers of the 'Holy Land' were called Saracens and included Arabs, Turks and Kurds. Their most famous leader was Salah-ed-din Yussuf ('Saladin', 1137-1193). He earned the respect of many Crusaders. Contact with Arab civilization opened the eyes of many Europeans to the wider world.

22

✤ 1066
Norman knights wear long
tunic of mail ('hauberk')

✤ 1099
The Order of the Knights of
St John is founded

✤ 1119
The Order of Knights Templar
is founded

✤ 1200s
Horses protected with
padded or mail coats called
trappers

✤ 1292
Statute of Arms lays down
rules for English tournaments

KNIGHTS IN ARMOUR

Knights might be away at the wars for
years on end. Castles and households
were often managed by their ladies.

I N the 700s, a simple invention had reached Europe
from Asia – stirrups. They supported the legs of a
horseback rider and made it possible for mounted
soldiers to charge the enemy really hard, without
falling. By Norman times, horse soldiers called knights
had become the most important part of most armies.
Even lords and kings had to learn how to be good
knights. In the 1100s and 1200s, almost every battlefield
shook to the thundering hooves of great war-horses
leading a cavalry charge.

HERALDRY

In a tournament or a battle, it was hard
to tell one armoured knight from
another. Knights began to use personal
badges or emblems, which were
displayed on surcoats (tunics worn over
armour), on shields and standards. These
emblems were passed down from one
generation of a family to another. They
became known as coats-of-arms and
can still be seen carved on castle stones
or coloured in the stained glass of old
churches. The rules for drawing up
coats-of-arms are known as heraldry.

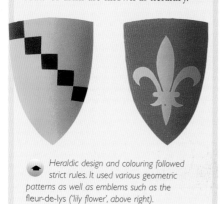

Heraldic design and colouring followed
strict rules. It used various geometric
patterns as well as emblems such as the
fleur-de-lys ('lily flower', above right).

A fine display
Fancy crests, plumes
and scarves were
worn at tournaments
to impress the
spectators.

Jousting helmet
The 'great helm' worn for
tournaments was padded
with straw.

Coats-of-arms
In tournaments and
battles even the
horses displayed
coats-of-arms.

THE AGE OF CHIVALRY

In the high Middle Ages, knights developed a code of
behaviour, called 'chivalry'. It was based on Christian
virtues. A knight vowed to protect the weak, honour
women, keep his word and respect his enemies. These
ideas were admired by many later generations, but
they were only ever an ideal. Battles may have had
strict rules, but they were still brutal affairs. Respect
was certainly not extended to peasants or to enemy
foot soldiers, who were slaughtered without mercy.

✤ **1300s**
'Coat of plates' – armoured plates stitched to tunics

✤ **1330s**
Solid breastplate encases the upper part of the body

✤ **1334**
Edward III of England founds knightly Order of the Garter

✤ **1400s**
Full plate armour covers whole body

✤ **c1490**
James IIII of Scotland founds knightly Order of the Thistle

23

Pauldrons
Shielded the shoulders from heavy blows.

Helmets
Now protected the whole face as well as the skull.

Gorgets
Were plates which prevented the throat being stabbed.

Breastplates
Covered the ribs.

Cowters
Covered the elbows.

Skirts
Plate strips protected the waist.

Gauntlets
Were jointed, armoured gloves.

Cuisses
Protected the thighs.

Poleyns
Protected the kneecaps.

Greaves
Protected the shins and lower leg.

Sabatons
Were pointed, armoured shoes.

◗ By the 1400s, plate armour encased the knight's whole body.

◗ Weapons used in hand-to-hand fighting included clubs (called 'maces') and all kinds of swords and daggers.

BECOMING A KNIGHT

Young boys started to learn how to be a knight at about the age of seven, when they were sent to serve as a page in a castle. They were taught to fight, ride and use weapons. At about 14 they became an esquire, or assistant to a knight, and could go into battle. At about 21, or earlier if they showed great courage, esquires would be made full knights.

Sword
A double-edged blade like this was used in the 1300s.

Mace
Knights used clubs like this one after about 1250.

SPLENDID TOURNAMENTS

More than 800 years ago, knights turned their military training into a sport. They fought mock battles called *mêlées* and later fought one-to-one, galloping at each other with lances raised. This was called jousting. It was a very violent sport and deaths were common. Grand competitons called tournaments were held, at which young knights sought fame and fortune. Before they took part, they dedicated their fight to a lady of the court.

◗ Two knights clash in a joust. After the 1400s, their horses would be separated by a low wooden fence called a tilt.

✤ cAD 950
Motte-and-bailey castles
built in France

✤ 1066
Normans bring castle
building to the British Isles

✤ 1100s
Castle defences centred on
massive stone towers called
keeps

✤ 1180s
Castles built with square wall
towers

✤ 1220s
Castles built with
round wall towers

THE AGE OF CASTLES

FORTRESSES had been built in Britain in Roman times. After the Normans invaded England in 1066, powerful kings and lords began to build new kinds of fortresses, called castles. Castles served as homes, as well as military bases and centres of government. They were used to control conquered lands and show off the power of their owner. Kings and lords sometimes owned several castles and moved from one to the other during the year.

The first castles were wooden towers called baileys, on top of earthen mounds called mottes. By the 1100s, castles were being built with thick stone walls.

LIFE IN A CASTLE

The centre of activity in the castle was the Great Hall. This was where banquets and important meetings were held. In the kitchens, meat sizzled on spits in front of the fire. The bedrooms and the main living room (called a 'solar') were often cold and draughty. Fresh reeds were strewn on the stone floors, as there were no carpets. There were rooms for the servants, guard rooms and stables.

During a siege, armed knights could ride out from 'sally ports' – small gates at the side of the castle – to launch a counter-attack.

Peasants worked the fields around the castle, supplying it with food. Grain was stored inside the castle walls, in case a siege cut off supplies.

HISTORIC CASTLES

Massive stone castles were built all over England, Wales, Scotland and Ireland. Many of them can still be seen today. Some of them are ruined, but you can still see the holes where joists once supported floors and timbers, or the arrow loops in the walls. Some castles are still in use as museums or private homes.

Edinburgh, Scotland, was fortified in ancient times. Parts of its castle date back to the 1000s.

✤ 1290s
Concentric castles, built with rings of walls and towers.

✤ 1320s
The age of gunpowder begins, new threat to castles

✤ 1350s
Bricks begin to be used in building some castles

✤ 1450s
Castles start to be replaced by fortified homes and palaces

✤ 1600s
Last military use of castles in British Isles

25

KING OF THE CASTLES

Beaumaris castle is on the Isle of Anglesey, in Wales. Work on it began in April 1295 and cost a fortune. It employed no fewer than 2,000 labourers, 200 stonemasons and 400 quarrymen. Beaumaris was the last in a powerful chain of castles built by King Edward I of England to secure his conquest of North Wales. He was the greatest castle builder of his day.

Stonemasons and carpenters were recruited from all over the Kingdom of England.

◆ Castles had to be strongly built and heavily defended to withstand attack.

SIEGE WARFARE

An army trying to attack a castle tried to surround it and cut off its supplies, so that the defenders starved. This was called a siege. Blazing arrows were shot into roof timbers. The walls were pounded with boulders from giant catapults, or undermined with tunnels dug beneath the foundations. More sieges ended by treaty or agreement than by the fall of the castle.

◆ The first cannon were very unreliable, but by the mid-1400s they were used to deadly effect.

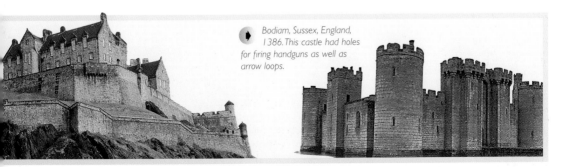

◆ Bodiam, Sussex, England, 1386. This castle had holes for firing handguns as well as arrow loops.

✤ 1080
Building of York Minster,
England

✤ 1136
Melrose Abbey, Scotland, is
built

✤ 1154
The only English pope,
Hadrian IV (to 1159)

✤ 1171
Pilgrimage to Canterbury
Cathedral begins

✤ 1172
Christchurch Cathedral,
Dublin

TO THE GLORY OF GOD

I N later medieval Europe, the
Christian faith was part of everday
life. It was expressed in the great
stone cathedrals and abbeys which were
raised all over the British Isles in the
Middle Ages. Building styles changed
over the years. Some cathedrals had
massive, awe-inspiring towers. Others
were graceful, with tall spires pointing
to heaven. Inside, gold glittered in
candle light and coloured ('stained')
glass windows glowed like precious gems.

Durham Cathedral, towering
above the River Wear in the
northeast of England, was started by
the Normans in 1093. It contains the
tombs of St Cuthbert and Bede. During
the Middle Ages the bishops of Durham
were as warlike as any barons and had
great political power.

In the Middle Ages, the language of
the Roman Church was Latin, which
few ordinary people could understand.
Most were unable to read either. Stained
glass windows were an ideal way of telling
worshippers stories from the Bible or the
lives of the saints.

✤ 1180
St David's Cathedral,
Wales, is rebuilt

✤ 1215
Roman Church and Pope at
height of power

✤ 1221
Friars enter England for
first time

✤ 1250
Westminster Abbey is rebuilt
near London

✤ 1380s
Bible first translated into the
English language

27

Monks and nuns lived
in monasteries and
convents. Some cared for the
sick or taught young people.
Some travelled from one town
to another, living on charity.
Religious orders such as the
Franciscans ('Grey Friars') or
the Dominicans ('Black Friars')
were founded in the 1200s.

MONKS AND NUNS

By about 1215 the Roman Church was at the height of
its power and wealth. It was at that time that an Italian
monk called Francis of Assisi called for Christians to
give up riches and help the poor and the sick. By the
1220s his ideas were being spread through the British
Isles by wandering monks, or friars. However many
church officials remained greedy and corrupt. They
were condemned by an English priest called John
Wycliffe, who gained many followers in the 1300s.

LETTERS OF GOLD

Before the days of printing, books had
to be copied out by hand. The work
was often done in monasteries. The
pages were made of vellum (animal
skin) and decorated with elaborate
letter designs and small pictures, called
'illuminations'. Books were such rare
and precious objects that they were
often chained to the shelf.

Illuminated
letters were
decorated
with coloured
paint and gold
leaf. They were
works of art
in themselves.

MYSTERIES AND MIRACLES

CANTERBURY PILGRIMS

Many people went on pilgrimage to
holy sites, such as the tomb of Thomas
Becket in Canterbury. They prayed for
healing or forgiveness of sins. Between
1387 and 1400 a poet called Geoffrey
Chaucer wrote about these pilgrims
and of the stories they told to pass the
time. The *Canterbury Tales* was one of
the first and greatest works of English
literature.

Many people believed in miracles or in the healing
power of relics such as saints' bones (which were
often fakes). Some Christians became hermits, living
alone to meditate. A woman called Julian of Norwich
wrote about the meaning of religious visions she had
in 1373. At that time a poem called *Piers Plowman*
was also written, which celebrated the simple faith of
ordinary people. The Bible was not translated into
English until the 1380s. One way people
could learn about the scriptures was
through acting. Religious ('mystery')
plays, featuring angels and devils, were
performed outside many cathedrals.

Amongst Chaucer's pilgrims were a
knight, a nun, monks, a miller, a lawyer,
a merchant and a doctor – a cross-section of
medieval society.

28

✤ 1063
Death of Gruffudd ap Llywelyn, having briefly united Wales

✤ c1115
Welsh princes start to build their own castles

✤ 1164
Founding of Strata Florida abbey (Ystrad Fflur)

✤ 1165
Owain Gwynedd resists Henry II of England

✤ 1176
Eisteddfod held at Cardigan Castle

THE WELSH PRINCES

WALES in the 1100s and 1200s was a rural land, with few large towns. People farmed and hunted, travelling by narrow tracks through the mountain passes. The princes were guarded by castles built by the Welsh rulers. They also endowed (funded) great monasteries such as Strata Florida (Ystrad Fflur) in the Teifi valley and Llanfaes, on Anglesey. There was a rich tradition of music, and a great gathering of poets (an *eisteddfod*) was held at Cardigan in 1176.

Rhys ap Grufudd ('the Lord Rhys' of Deheubarth) weakened Norman power in South Wales during the chaotic reign of King Stephen in England.

WHO HOLDS POWER?

Under rulers such as Rhys ap Gruffudd in the south and Owain Gwynedd in the north, Norman power in Wales declined. The Marcher Lords still held the borders, however, and the English kings regarded themselves as overlords of the Welsh. The division of Wales into separate kingdoms played into the hands of the English. In 1157 Madog ap Maredudd of Powys helped King Henry II of England invade Wales, in order to weaken his rivals in Gwynedd.

St David's Cathedral came under the control of Norman bishops in 1115. It was rebuilt in 1182.

GERALD OF WALES

Gerald de Barri was born in about 1146. His ancestry was part Norman, part Welsh. Gerald became a talented writer in Latin and a great churchman. In 1188 he travelled through Wales with Archbishop Baldwin, and his *Journey Through Wales* and *Description of Wales* give us lively and good-humoured pictures of Wales in the high Middle Ages. He died in 1223 and has gone down in history as Giraldus Cambriensis, or Gerald of Wales.

✤ **1188**
Gerald de Barri travels through Wales

✤ **1216**
Llywelyn Fawr summons parliament at Aberdyfi

✤ **1250**
Coal being mined at Margam, in South Wales

✤ **1267**
English recognize Llywelyn ap Gruffudd as Prince of Wales

✤ **1283**
Llywelyn ap Gruffudd killed in skirmish with English, Cilmeri

29

RULERS IN WALES

✤ Gruffudd ap Llywelyn   1039-1063
✤ Bleddyn ap Cynfyn   1063-75
✤ Trahaearn ap Caradog   1075-1081
✤ Gruffudd ap Cynan   1081-1137
✤ Owain Gwynedd   1137-1170
✤ Dafydd ap Owain Gwynedd 1170-1194
✤ Llywelyn 'Fawr' ('the Great') 1194-1240
✤ Dafydd ap Llywelyn   1240-1246
✤ Llywelyn ap Gruffudd   1246-1282

Llywelyn II's death near Cilmeri in 1282 marked the end of Welsh independence. He is remembered in Wales as 'The Last Prince'.

THE GREAT LLYWELYN

In 1170 three sons of Owain Gwynedd fought each other at Pentraeth, on Anglesey, for the throne of Gwynedd. Hywel was defeated by Rhodri and Dafydd and the kingdom was divided. By 1194 all Gwynedd had come under the rule of Llywelyn ap Iorwerth, 'the Great'. Llywelyn married Joan or Siwan, daughter of King John of England, but the two rulers later became enemies. Llywelyn was the most powerful ruler in medieval Wales, a strong supporter of the Church and the law.

This stone head is believed to represent Llywelyn Fawr, 'the Great'. He held court at Aberffraw, on Anglesey.

THE LAST PRINCE

Llywelyn was succeeded by his younger son, Dafydd, but he died in the sixth year of his reign. He was to be followed by his nephews Llywelyn and Owain, but the former seized the throne for himself and gained control of all Wales. Llywelyn II ap Gruffudd was recognized as Prince of Wales by the English in 1267. However he would be the last Welsh prince. He quarelled with King Edward I and after long wars, was killed in a skirmish with English troops near Cilmeri. His severed head was displayed in London.

THE CONQUEST

King Edward I of England was now the undisputed ruler of Wales. His castles ringed the land. English criminal laws replaced Welsh ones and the *Statute of Rhuddlan* (1284) divided Wales into counties, along English lines. In 1301 Edward I's son (the later Edward II) was declared Prince of Wales, and ever since then the title has been held by the eldest son of the English monarch.

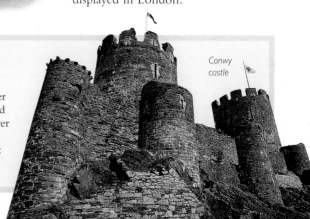

Conwy castle

✤ 1130s
Norman families gain estates in the Lowlands

✤ 1174
William I of Scotland forced to recognize English king as overlord

✤ 1264
Norwegian invasion defeated at Largs

✤ 1266
Scotland gains Norwegian territories on mainland and Western Isles

✤ 1296
Edward I of England defeats John Balliol at Dunbar

SCOTTISH FREEDOM

I N the 1100s, Scotland saw great changes. Norman families gained Scottish lands. Three sons of the great Queen Margaret ruled the country in turn – Edgar, Alexander I and the great David I. Many fine churches and abbeys were built during their reigns, and around them developed prosperous 'burghs' (large towns). Peasants lived in small farming villages called 'touns'.

RULERS OF SCOTLAND

✤ Donald III Bán	1093–1097
✤ Duncan II	1094
✤ Edgar	1097–1107
✤ Alexander I 'the Fierce'	1107–1124
✤ David I 'the Saint'	1124–1153
✤ Malcolm IV 'the Maiden'	1153–1165
✤ William I 'the Lion'	1165–1214
✤ Alexander II	1214–1229
✤ Alexander III	1249–1286
✤ Margaret 'Maid of Norway'	1286–1290
✤ Throne disputed	1290–1292
✤ John (Balliol)	1292–1296
✤ Edward I of England	1296–1306

House of Bruce

✤ Robert I Bruce	1306–1329
✤ David II	1329–1371
✤ Edward Balliol	1306 & 1333–1336

SCOTLAND STANDS FIRM

In 1174, William I of Scotland was captured by English troops and forced to recognize Henry II as his overlord. It was an act never forgotten by the English – or the Scots. Alexander III, who came to the throne as a boy, had another old enemy to deal with – Norway. The Norwegians invaded in 1263, but were forced to withdraw and finally lost their mainland and island territories.

David I was succeeded by his young son Malcolm IV, who died before he was married.

✤ 1297
William Wallace defeats
English army at Stirling Bridge

✤ 1305
William Wallace captured and
executed

✤ 1314
English defeated by Robert
Bruce at Bannockburn

✤ 1328
England recognizes Scotland
as independent

✤ 1371
Rule of Scotland passes to
the Stewarts

31

SCOTLAND FALLS

Tragedy now struck the Scots. In 1286 Alexander III fell from
his horse and was killed. Four years later his successor, the
young girl Margaret of Norway, also died. Who should reign
next, was unclear. The Scots turned to Edward I of England for
advice. His candidate was John Balliol, a distant descendant of
David I. Edward I thought he could control his chosen man,
but instead Balliol turned and made an historic alliance with
France. Edward I stormed into Scotland in 1296 and defeated
Balliol at Dunbar.

William Wallace blocked
the northern advance of
English forces at Stirling Bridge in
1297 and became Edward I's
most hated foe.

LORDS OF THE ISLES

In the Highlands and Western
Isles, the old Gaelic way of
life continued. Here, first
loyalty was to the chief of the
clan (a group sharing descent
from a common ancestor).
The lands of Clans Dugall,
Donald and Ruairi became
known as the Lordship of the
Isles. The first Lord of the
Isles was John of Islay of Clan
Donald, who died in 1387.
The Lordship was in constant
conflict with the Scottish
kingdom and was brought to
an end in 1493.

Legend has it
that Robert
Bruce was inspired to
keep fighting the
English by watching a
spider try time after
time to rebuild its web.
At last it succeeded.
Bannockburn was the
turning point, although
the war continued for
another 14 years.

WAR OF INDEPENDENCE

Resistance to English rule was fierce. Its champion was
William Wallace, who defeated an English army at
Stirling Bridge, but was himself defeated at Falkirk in
1298. Captured in 1305, Wallace was horribly executed
in London. Parts of his body were sent to Newcastle,
Berwick, Stirling and Perth. The fight was taken up by
Robert Bruce (who had stabbed his chief rival, John
Comyn, to death). Robert was crowned king by the
Scots in 1306. Edward I died in the following year and
at Bannockburn, on 24 June 1314, Bruce turned the
tide and defeated 20,000 troops of Edward II.

32

✤ 1175
Treaty of Windsor. Rory
O'Connor recognizes Henry
II as overlord.

✤ 1210
Irish kings submit to King
John of England

✤ 1235
Normans complete conquest
of western Ireland

✤ 1257
Irish attack Normans in Sligo
and Thomond

✤ 1315
Edward Bruce invades
Ireland from Scotland

THE PALE AND BEYOND

THE word 'pale' means fence or enclosure. In medieval Ireland it came to mean the area of the country which was directly controlled by the kings of England. It lay in the east of the country, around Dublin. Within the Pale, English language, laws, fashions, architecture and customs became normal. The Pale was settled not just by English royal officials, but by merchants and labourers too, from across the Irish Sea.

THE ENGLISH PALE IN IRELAND

ULSTER
CONNAUGHT
Louth
Meath
THE PALE
Kildare
Dublin
LEINSTER
Limerick
MUNSTER
Waterford
Wexford
Cork
IRISH SEA

◐ The Breac Maedhóc is a bronze shrine from Drumlane, County Kavan. Its figures show the Gaels of Ireland in the 1100s. The men have long hair and beards and wear long cloaks. The women wear their hair in ringlets.

◑ The area of the Pale varied greatly during the later Middle Ages. By 1464 it included the counties of Dublin, Kildare, Louth and Meath.

THREE WORLDS, ONE LAND

Beyond the Pale, lay the lands of two other groups – the Irish-speaking Gaels and the powerful, independent Norman families who had seized Irish land. Over the years, many of the latter adopted Irish ways. The English kings, however, firmly believed that civilization ended 'beyond the Pale'. This phrase is still sometimes used today to describe unacceptable or uncouth behaviour. From time to time the English attempted to expand their rule by founding colonies beyond the Pale. These were English settlements protected by soldiers.

THE STATUTES OF KILKENNY

From the early days of English rule in Ireland, the official policy was one of separation and apartness. In 1366 the English, under Prince Lionel of Clarence, called a parliament at Kilkenny and passed a wide range of statutes (laws).

According to these, English colonists were not allowed to marry into Irish families, or to adopt Irish dress or customs. They were not to speak Irish or use the ancient Irish legal system, known as Brehon Law.

✤ 1318
Edward Bruce killed at Battle of Faughart

✤ 1320
University founded in Dublin, first in Ireland

✤ 1333
English crown loses control of Connaught and Ulster

✤ 1366
Statutes of Kilkenny are proclaimed

✤ 1394
Richard II of England regains control of Ireland

33

BARLEY FOR THE TAKING

When Henry II of England landed in Ireland in 1171, his chief aim had been to make sure that 'Strongbow' and his adventurers did not set up a Norman kingdom in Ireland to rival his own. As the years went by, the English found another reason for staying in Ireland. The lush, green pastures and fields of ripe barley were a valuable economic resource. Grain from Irish estates could be exported to England or mainland Europe for rich rewards.

KERN AND GALLOGLASS

Ireland saw wave after wave of English invasion. John came in 1185 as prince and again in 1210 as king. Richard II arrived in 1394-1395 and again in 1399. There were long battles between the old Norman families and amongst the Irish kings. By recognizing the English kings, some Irish royal families managed to survive and even thrive in this changing world. The poor peasants experienced endless warfare. All sides used roving bands of troops who would fight for anyone who paid and fed them. These mercenaries included Norman men-at-arms, Irish footsoldiers called kerns and Scottish adventurers called galloglass, meaning 'foreign warriors'.

The Rock of Cashel is crowned by splendid buildings from the Middle Ages. Cormac's Chapel dates from 1127-34, while the great cathedral was built about 100 years later.

These stone carved tombs represent two of Ireland's most powerful families at the close of the Middle Ages. They may be seen in St Canice's Cathedral, Kilkenny. They belong to Piers Butler, Earl of Ossory and Ormond, and his wife Lady Margaret Fitzgerald.

34

✦ c1170
Major period of
town building begins

✦ 1176
London Bridge is
rebuilt in stone

✦ 1233
Piped water supply to
Westminster, near London

✦ 1250s
Zoo animals including lions in
Tower of London

✦ c1300
Town building starts to decline

A MEDIEVAL TOWN

Towns were now beginning to grow quickly. They were noisy, rowdy places and often foul-smelling, too, for there was no proper drainage. Water had to be carried to each house from wells. Carts brought vegetables to market and cattle were herded though the muddy streets. Women tied wooden platforms called pattens to their shoes, to walk through the puddles. Travellers slept huddled together on straw mattreses, in flea-infested inns.

🔺 *Rich merchants began to build with stone. The Jew's House in Lincoln is over 800 years old and has a hall on the first floor.*

WALLS AND CHIMNEYS

Medieval cities were surrounded by walls and at night the gates were locked and barred. Tall wooden-framed houses were crowded together. House fires were common and straw thatch was often banned in favour of slates and tiles, which could not blaze. All cooking fires had to be covered each night – the time of 'curfew' (from the Old French *cuevre-feu*). At first smoke came out through holes in the wall. It was not until the 1400s that chimney pots topped the roofs.

◀ *By the 1250s, most of the English population lived within 25 kilometres of a market town. Modern cities that were founded during the Middle Ages include Liverpool, Hull, Leeds, Newcastle upon Tyne, Portsmouth.*

Timber houses
In the Middle Ages, most houses were still built with timber frames and walls of wattle-and-daub. Some of these may still be seen in Britain today.

Open sewers
Waste was thrown into the street and streams were used as open sewers. Birds and dogs scavenged rubbish tips.

✤ c1350
Average town has a
population of about 3,000

✤ c1350
Rapid growth in the woollen
cloth trade

✤ 1411
Guildhall rebuilt in the City
of London

✤ 1463
First record of eating with
forks in Britain

✤ 1463
Playing cards in use
in Britain

35

OLD LONDON BRIDGE

The first versions of London Bridge were made of wood, and they really did keep falling down, just as it says in the old nursery rhyme. However a 19-arch stone bridge, built between 1176 and 1209, lasted until 1831. On this bridge there were rows of houses and even a chapel. Sometimes the bridge was used for jousting. Traitors' heads were often displayed on the bridge after they had been chopped off.

The wealth of merchants began to compete with that of the nobles and the Church.

MONEY AND MERCHANTS

Merchants became wealthy. In London there were great warehouses owned by the Hanseatic League, a powerful organization which traded right across Germany to the Baltic Sea. Bankers lent money in return for payment of interest. Even kings borrowed from them to pay for their wars. When bankers became richer than kings, it was clear that the old feudal system was breaking down. Craft workers formed trading guilds which controlled the marketing of their wares. Young lads came to stay in the house of the master of their trade and learned how to be a weaver, a tailor or a goldsmith. They were called apprentices.

Shop signs
When most people people couldn't read, shop signs had to be visual. A boot might hang above a cobbler's shop, or a horse-shoe above a smithy. A green bush was the sign of an inn.

Animals to market
Even large cities echoed to the sound of cattle, sheep and geese being driven through the streets to market.

FOOTBALL HOOLIGANS

Apprentices were an unruly lot and often tried to avoid work. They formed gangs on the streets. One of their favourite sports was football. A blown-up pig's bladder served as a ball. There were no rules and the game was played on the street. It was very rough. In 1314 the sport was banned by King Edward II of England.

36

❋ 1314
Weather destroys harvests, major famine

❋ 1315
Harvests fail yet again, starvation

❋ 1348
Black Death appears in England and Wales

❋ 1349
Black Death reaches Scotland, kills one in five

❋ 1351
England attempts to freeze workers' wages

THE HARD LÍFE

O N 14 April 1360 the weather was so foul and bitter that many horseback riders were reported to have died of cold, frozen to death in their saddles. There were few comforts in the Middle Ages. Castles were draughty and stank of sewage from the cesspit or the moat. People rarely bathed and disease was common. Many women never survived childbirth and children often died when small.

MEDIEVAL MEDICINE
Medical knowledge had grown little since the days of the Romans. Surgeons could mend bones and monks grew herbs to make medicines. Some of these cures worked, but many didn't. One common treatment was bleeding – taking blood from the patient.

A leper's clapper

"OUR DAILY BREAD"
While the nobles ate fine wheaten bread, the poor ate crusts of coarse rye. Rye crops were sometimes spoiled by a fungus disease called ergot. People who ate flour made from mouldy rye became sick and saw strange visions. Country people preserved their own food, salting fish and smoking bacon. They ate eggs and caught hares and waterfowl. If the harvests failed and prices rose, then people starved.

Food supply was seasonal and depended on good harvests. Famine was common.

Leprosy was an infectious disease. Lepers had to carry a wooden clapper, to warn people that they were coming along the road.

SINNERS AND LEPERS
Natural disasters and illnesses were often believed to be punishments sent by God, because of human sinfulness. One of the most feared diseases was leprosy, which causes lumps, discoloured patches and ulcers to form on the body. Fingers and toes would sometimes become numb and fall off. Sufferers (lepers) were banned from public places and were only allowed to watch church services through a slit in the wall.

Rats and fleas were all too common in medieval towns and cities. The plague was first brought to England by the black rats which used to infest almost every ship.

✤ 1361
A second outbreak of the
plague in Britain

✤ 1369
A third outbreak of the plague
in Britain

✤ 1377
Poll tax introduced in
England

✤ 1381
Peasants' Revolt in England led
by Wat Tyler

✤ 1390
The plague returns for the
fourth time

37

THE BLACK DEATH

In August 1348 a new disease appeared at the port of Weymouth, in the southwest of England. It was known as the Pestilence, later as the Black Death. This terrible plague, spread by rats and their fleas, had already devastated Central Asia and Europe. Soon it was raging across England, Wales, Scotland and Ireland. The Black Death took various forms. One poisoned the bloodstream and caused horrid swellings and boils on the body. Another affected the lungs and could be passed on by coughing and sneezing.

◗ In medieval Europe, knowledge of diseases and medicine had not advanced since Roman times. The sick were sometimes cared for by nuns. The Black Death killed many of the carers as well as the patients. Soon, plague victims were being buried in mass graves and there were no priests left to pray for their souls.

A LABOUR SHORTAGE

In the years 1347 to 1351, the plague may have killed 75 million people in Asia and Europe. Many villages in the British Isles lost half to two-thirds of their population. In some there were no survivors at all. There was a great shortage of labour, so workers now found that they could demand high wages. The English government passed harsh laws in a desperate bid to keep wages at the same level, in 1349 and 1351.

THE PEASANTS' REVOLT

In England after 1377, people had to pay more and more poll taxes (standard payments demanded from all citizens). In 1381 angry peasants from Kent and Essex, led by Wat Tyler and a priest called John Ball, stormed London. Fourteen year old King Richard II rode out to meet the rebels and offered to take up their cause. But Wat Tyler was cut down by the Mayor of London and the rising was savagely suppressed.

◀ Twenty thousand peasants marched on London in 1381. They burnt the palace of John of Gaunt, Duke of Lancaster. They killed the archbishop, captured the Tower of London and set prisoners free.

38

✦ 1337
Edward III of England declares
himself King of France

✦ 1340
Naval battle off Sluys won by
England

✦ 1346
English defeat the French at
Crécy

✦ 1347
English troops capture the
French port of Calais

✦ 1356
The Black Prince defeats the
French at Poitiers

THE HUNDRED YEARS' WAR

T HE period we know as the Hundred Years' War was a long drawn out, bloody struggle between England and France. It took place across the muddy battlefields of northern France and Flanders (in what is now Belgium). It was never really one war, but a series of raids, battles, campaigns and treaties. Nor did it last 100 years, but from 1337 until 1453.

WHO RULES FRANCE?

King Edward III of England was related to the French royal family and in 1337 he claimed the throne of France as his own. England had fought for its lands in France ever since the days of the Normans and the Angevin empire. What was more, France was now a close ally of Scotland, England's enemy. The result was a war which cost Edward III's subjects dearly. They had to pay for it with taxes, loss of trade – and their lives.

Edward 'the Black Prince', was the eldest son of Edward III. His nickname came from the colour of his armour. Edward was a brilliant soldier who made a name for himself when he was only 16, at the Battle of Crécy. In 1356 he won a great victory at Poitiers. He died in 1376.

In October 1415, Henry V found his route blocked by a huge French army (foreground) at the village of Agincourt. His 6,000 troops were sick with dysentery and greatly outnumbered, but he won a great victory. The French knights became bogged down in mud, while flight after flight of arrows whistled through the air.

The crossbow was a much more accurate weapon than the ordinary bow.

WEAPONS AND TACTICS

For campaign after campaign, the English raided and plundered northern France. Long columns of battle-weary knights, waggons, footsoldiers and archers trailed across the countryside. Some carried new-fangled handguns, others hauled early cannon. When it came to pitched battles, England's great strength lay in its use of archers, armed with deadly longbows. They could fire up to 12 arrows a minute.

✤ 1360
The Peace of Brétigny between England and France

✤ 1415
Henry V of England wins the battle of Agincourt

✤ 1420
The *Treaty of Troyes*. Henry V becomes heir to the French throne

✤ 1431
The English burn Joan of Arc as a witch at Rouen

✤ 1453
English defeat at Castillon, end of the 100 Years' War

39

THE GAME OF CHESS

The English were not alone in their attacks on the French kings. At times they were allied with the Bretons of the northwest, at times with powerful barons from Burgundy, in the east. At first the English achieved some great victories. At Poitiers in 1356 the French king, Jean II ('the Good'), was captured. Three years later, the *Treaty of Brétigny* offered Edward III one-third of France if he gave up his claims to the throne.

THE TABLES ARE TURNED

Peace did not last. When Henry V came to the throne of England, he led his army back across the Channel and was victorious. In 1420 the *Treaty of Troyes* made him heir to the French throne – but within two years he was dead. French fortunes now began to turn. Their knights were inspired by a peasant girl called Joan of Arc. She claimed that voices of the saints had called her to free her homeland. The English accused her of witchcraft and burned her alive in 1431. However by 1453 France had regained most of the English-occupied lands.

"DEAR KATE"

In Shakespeare's play *Henry V*, she is called 'dear Kate'. 'Kate' was Catherine de Valois, daughter of Charles VI of France. In 1420 she married Henry V of England, at the height of his success, but her husband became sick while away at the wars and died in 1422. Nine years later, Catherine secretly married a handsome young Welsh courtier. His name was Owain Tudur or Tudor, and it was their grandson, Henry VII, who founded the most famous dynasty in English history.

Catherine de Valois married Henry V at Troyes. She was crowned Queen of England and gave birth to a son, the future Henry VI, in 1421. Her eldest son by Owain Tudor was Edmund, Earl of Richmond, and he was father to Henry VII, the first Tudor monarch.

40

✤ 1296
The Welsh Revolt under
Madog ap Llywelyn

✤ 1316
Llywelyn Bren revolts in South
Wales

✤ 1369
Owain Lawgoch gains support
in France

✤ 1400
Owain Glyndwr rises against
English rule

✤ 1403
Welsh and English rebels
defeated at Shrewsbury

THE WELSH RISE UP

Wales was changing under English rule. Towns had already been developing in the days of the Welsh princes. Now, new shire or county towns controlled all local trade, and they prospered. In the Welsh heartlands, the new towns took the form of colonies, settled by incomers from England, France or Flanders. Welsh citizens were often forcibly removed to other settlements.

TROUBLED TIMES

Many Welsh people protested against the taxes and laws brought in by the English. An uprising began in 1294, led by Madog ap Llywelyn, but it was put down in 1295. In 1317 there was a revolt in South Wales, led by Llywelyn Bren. Perhaps the greatest danger to English rule came from Owain Lawgoch, grandson of Llywelyn Fawr. He fought as a mercenary for the French, who called him Yvain de Galles. He planned to reconquer Wales with French help, but was murdered by a secret agent in 1378.

Harlech Castle, completed by King Edward I of England in 1289, was besieged and captured by Owain Glyndŵr's rebels in the spring of 1404. It remained in Welsh hands until 1409.

Love and life in fourteenth century Wales is described in the poems of Dafydd ap Gwilym.

POET OF LOVE AND NATURE

Dafydd ap Gwilym is believed by many to be the greatest ever writer in the Welsh language. He was born in the parish of Llanbadarn Fawr, near Aberystwyth, and wrote his masterpieces between 1320 and 1370. He broke with traditional Welsh verse forms and was influenced by French literature. Dafydd wrote light-hearted and joyful poems, many of them about his sweethearts, Morfudd and Dyddgu. He wrote about nature, too, describing the grace of a seagull's flight in a way that still seems very modern today.

✚ 1404
Owain Glyndŵr summons
first of three parliaments

✚ 1404
Welsh treaty with Charles VI
of France

✚ 1408
English start to regain
control of Wales

✚ 1413
The end of the Welsh
uprising, English rule restored

✚ 1415
Owain Glyndŵr goes into
hiding and disappears

41

A SPARK CATCHES FIRE

In 1400 Lord Grey of Ruthin, a personal friend of the English king, Henry IV, seized some land from his neighbour in the Marches of northeast Wales. Owain Glyndŵr was a middle-aged Welsh nobleman of royal descent. He appealed to the English parliament for justice, but they reacted with contempt, declaring the Welsh to be 'barefoot rascals'. A simple land dispute rapidly became a full-scale national uprising. Owain was supported by all ranks of Welsh society, including monks and bishops. Welsh labourers and students hurried back from England to join him.

The longbow was a deadly weapon in the hands of Welsh archers.

Owain Glyndŵr had studied law in London and fought with the English army, but he now became leader of a Welsh uprising. He summoned Welsh parliaments at Machynlleth and Dolgellau.

THIRTEEN YEARS OF WAR

Owain was declared Prince of Wales and by 1401 most of his country had joined the uprising. Castles were captured and towns were sacked. Owain joined forces with rebel English barons Henry Percy ('Hotspur') and Edmund Mortimer, but they were defeated at Shrewsbury in 1403. Owain was also supported by the Scots and the French, who sent troops to support him. By 1408, the English were regaining control, but resistance continued until 1413.

MASTERS OF THE LONGBOW

Welsh archers are said to have been the first to develop the longbow. Unlike the shorter Norman bow, it was the full height of a man. It was normally made of yew and had a pull of about 40 kilograms. Arrows were about 78 cm long, made of ash with long metal tips. Goose-feather flights made them spin as they flew through the air. They could even pierce armour. The English used companies of Welsh archers to devastating effect during the Hundred Years' War with France.

42

✤ 1399
Henry IV, son of John of
Gaunt, is first Lancastrian king

✤ 1453
Henry VI suffers from mental
illness

✤ 1454
Richard, Duke of York
appointed Protector

✤ 1455
Battle of St Albans. Wars of
the Roses begin

✤ 1461
Edward of York is proclaimed
King of England

WARS ⊙F THE ROSES

As battle-hardened soldiers returned from the French wars, many entered the service of powerful English lords. Their job was to bully peasants for payment of taxes, or to fight in private armies. There was no shortage of work for them. For thirty years, from 1455 until 1485, there were civil wars as rival branches of the royal family fought for the throne of England.

◖ A red rose stood
for the House of
Lancaster. A white rose
was the badge of the
House of York. When
Henry VII came to the
throne, he combined
both designs in a red-
and-white 'Tudor rose'.

Lancaster

York

ENGLISH KINGS

House of Lancaster
✤ Henry IV   1399-1413
✤ Henry V   1413-1422
✤ Henry VI   1422-1461 & 1470-1471

House of York
✤ Edward IV   1461-1470 & 1471-1483
✤ Edward V   1483
✤ Richard III   1483-1485

House of Tudor
✤ Henry VII   1485-150

LANCASTER AND YORK

The Houses of Lancaster and York were both descended from Edward III. Their rivalry came to a head when a Lancastrian king, Henry VI, became too mentally ill to rule. In 1454 Richard, Duke of York, was appointed Protector. When Henry VI got better, Richard would not give up his new-found power, and went to war. Henry VI was defeated at St Albans in 1455, but then Richard was killed at Wakefield in 1460.

◖ There was a great battle
at Barnet, to the north
of London, on 14 April 1471.
Edward IV regained the throne
and killed his former ally,
Warwick 'the Kingmaker'.

✤ **1470**
Henry VI restored as King
of England

✤ **1471**
Lancastrians led by Queen
Margaret defeated at
Tewkesbury

✤ **1483**
Young Edward V and his
brother disappear

✤ **1483**
Parliament asks Richard of
Gloucester to become king

✤ **1485**
Henry Tudor defeats Richard
III at Bosworth

43

WARWICK 'THE KINGMAKER'

The most powerful man in England at this time was not
the weak king, but Richard Neville, Earl of Warwick. It was
he who had Richard's son proclaimed Edward IV in 1461,
the first Yorkist king. Henry VI was imprisoned and exiled.
Later, Warwick fell out with Edward and brought Henry VI
back to the throne. No wonder he was remembered in
history as the 'kingmaker'. Edward returned to seek revenge.
Warwick was killed in battle and Henry was murdered in
the Tower of London in 1471.

WHO MURDERED THE PRINCES?

Did Richard III murder the
princes in the Tower? He had
every reason to. Skeletons were
found in the Tower in 1674 and
buried in Westminster Abbey.
However some historians believe
that Richard III was not such a
villain as he is often made out to
be. Might Henry VII have been
the true murderer?

THE AGE OF PRINTING

In 1471 an Englishman called William
Caxton travelled to the German city of
Cologne. There he learned about a new
technology, which had been invented in
China and developed in Germany and
the Netherlands. It was called printing,
and it would change the world.
Caxton set up his own printing press at
Westminster in 1476
and produced about 100 titles.

THE MARCH TO BOSWORTH

Edward IV died in 1483. His heir, Edward V, was too
young to rule for himself, so he and his young brother
were left in the care of their uncle, Richard of
Gloucester. They went to live in the Tower of London,
but mysteriously, were never seen again. Gloucester was
crowned Richard III in the same year, at the request of
parliament. He did not rule for long. In 1485 the Earl
of Richmond, a Lancastrian, landed in Wales. His name
was Henry Tudor and he defeated and killed Richard
III at the battle of Bosworth, near Leicester. Henry VII
married Elizabeth of York, and brought peace and
prosperity to England.

THE MEDIEVAL CASTLE

Castles were built with rings of defences and were hard to attack. They were garrisoned by footsoldiers, archers and men-at-arms.

Arrow loops
Archers could shoot arrows through loops, narrow slits in the castle walls.

Outer walls
Thick stone walls were fireproof and hard to knock down.

Battlements
The walls were topped by battlements. These walk-ways were defended by stone blocks called merlons and firing gaps called crenels.

Machicolations
Chutes overhung the outer walls, for dropping missiles on the enemy.

Gatehouse
A strong gate called a portcullis could be dropped to seal off the entrance to the castle.

index

Look up subjects to be found in this book.
Illustrations are shown in *italic* print.

ACKN⊙WLEDGEMENTS

The publishers would like to thank the following sources for the use of their images:

Page 11 (B/R) Pavel Libera/Corbis; 16 (T/R) Leonard de Selva/Corbis; 26 (T/R) Archivo Iconografico/Corbis; 27 (B/L) Mary Evans Picture Library; 28 (B) Adam Woolfitt/Corbis; 31 (B/R) Bob Krist/Corbis; 34 (T/L) Lincolnshire County Council; 35 (T/R) Bridgeman Art Library; 37 (B/L) Bettmann/Corbis; 40 (T/R) Dean Conger/Corbis

All other photographs from MKP Archives

The publishers would like to thank the artists whose work appears in this book:

Julie Banyard, Richard Berridge/SpecsArt, Vanessa Card, Nicholas Forder, Peter Gregory, Alan Hancocks, Sally Holmes, Richard Hook/Linden Artists, Janos Marffy, Angus McBride/LindenArtists, Terry Riley, Martin Sanders, Peter Sarson, Rob Sheffield, Guy Smith/Mainline, Studio Galante, Rudi Vizi, Mike White/Temple Rogers